# No Lace Fronts in Iowa City

Poems

# No Lace Fronts in Iowa City

Poems

Meghan Malachi

Lake Dallas, Texas

Printed in the United States of America

FIRST EDITION

Requests for permission to reprint or reuse material
from this work should be sent to:

Permissions
Madville Publishing
PO Box 358
Lake Dallas, TX 75065

Cover Art: "A Wig for My Chair" by Mary Joak
Cover Design: Jacqueline Davis
Author Photo: Varya Bazalev

ISBN: 978-1-963695-69-4 paperback
978-1-963695-70-0 ebook
Library of Congress Control Number: 2026932782

*To my mother, my grandmothers, and all the women*
*who have poured into me*

*In memory of Judith Howell-Malachi*

# Contents

# Girl, I—

love you
to the dominican republic
and back. from the grease
your mother palms into
the only mangú i'll ever eat
to the folding chair you save
for me at the back of the church
behind the altar. from the dive
karaoke bar in southern florida,
where we shouted rap songs
into each other's mouths like
sustenance, where we shouted
rap songs to white people
who told us we were stars—to
fiji, where we never did make
that trip. from your 6 train to
my 5. from the braider on your
block to the beauty supply on
mine. from my bumped ends
to your cupped bang—our
foreheads matching in sweat
and sheen. from daddy issues
to resentment. from luis to jayson
from pablo to stephen from
jonathan to christopher and
all the other boys who didn't
love us back. from sandra
to natasha from rosa to gloria
from melissa to jazmine and all
the other women who loved us
full. from the day you
became kin,
named my cousins yours,
called my grandma, grandma
to the day you stopped calling home.
if i pried me open—there you'd be,

girl,
a blooming cell
a lingering clot
unmoved in the rush
of my waiting vessel.

## 21 Years

with a head bop to "New Thang" by French Montana and Remy Ma

what a blessing
to be from the city
that gave us
belcalis
& in part, luther vandross
& alfredo thiebaud, who soothed our grandparents' homesickness
with fresh coco while others feared their hunger
& adolescent mouths crutched on *mad* and *odee*
& a tongue that makes us say *ball* like one of hair is rolling up and
out of our throats
& cardi
& chairback clashing after high school graduations at the pine
& tall stacks at pelham bay diner
& kerry
& remy
& the payless on southern boulevard that's been goin out of business
for a decade
& the conway on hunts point that we ambled with our grandmas
and bought $3 panties from
& the bodega cashiers who watched us grow up as we watched them
grow old
& a hospital we were taught to trust with bullet wounds and nothing else
& deli windows plastered with high-definition shots of food you've
never actually seen inside
& a credibility that has us lookin sideways at anyone who claims to
be from the hood
& a knowing that celebration is in order at the uttering of *vamo pa
city island?*
& lesandro
& bodies leaned back for days
& a beach built for us, rebuilt for the city
& a beach named by the city, renamed by us
& a beach with a story we loathe but tell with a light which is
undeniable and which is ours.

## Where does your love come from?

after a prompt from Ariana Brown

My love comes from a small church in the South Bronx. It comes from a crate of water bottles sitting on the altar, the hands of choir girls digging to soothe scratchy throats. My love comes from Sandra's harmonies, a rising and falling prayer to God. She tells me my voice is something good. Demands I use it.

My love comes from my grandmother, who dresses us in her clothing to remind us we are foolish & small. My love comes from my grandmother, who scratches our thighs through the rips in our jeans, mends our sour bellies with soup on hot days, asks *why did you crucify your body?* when new piercings emerge from my cousin's nose, lip, lobe.

My love seeps from any hands that have touched my head, pressed oil into my scalp, guided butter into breakage, soap into knots. My love accepts the promise of symmetry with the parting of a pointed comb—it doesn't care to know what's real and what isn't. My love nestles into the hands that tuck strands into strands, color into curl, water into shine.

## Main Character

*You're having a main character moment,* baby girl says as I stare out the car window at blurred palm trees & Tampa lights splitting through the bridge. *Where else am I supposed to look?* I'm defensive but curious. She doesn't answer, only laughs & yells out to the other girls, *Y'all, this bitch having a main character moment!*

Dark tequila & Mama's garlic pork swish in our systems & we call each other beautiful & bitches & we celebrate being single & kind of single & the city shouts that we smell bold & electric—sweet, even. & we say *duh* & we say *of course we do* & I flush at all the times I must have been having a main character moment & didn't even know it.

How would I know it?
So many times I've looked out the window—this same window—& felt both full of hope & destroyed by hope. At once close to beautiful & as far away from beauty & its lies as I needed to be. I didn't even consider the stage I was setting, the cast I'd built around me. I shut my eyes, let the wet air crack through my beaming summer of a face. I am so sick of my face. Of this face crafted so gently by ancestry's bad calculus. How would I know it? Every girl in this car has been a victim of something. Every girl in this car has given more than they've taken, has taken more than any script would ever permit. Every girl in this car has told me *you deserve better* even when I am the villain & I wish that they, too, could sit in the thrill of being above heroism.

## Proof

When I was a mathematician
I slept three hours each night
with dreams of abelian groups
and algebraic closures. My
gums peeled till dawn, enamel
crushed from terrors that the
last theorem I proved might
curve in on itself, that another
infinity could be hiding in the
trivial. Since dropping out, I
haven't thought about
mathematics. By this I mean
moonless nights are now
plagued only by bills,
indigestion, the poems
swimming in my gut. I mean:
I wake up already so full of
the morning. I mean: I take
Galois for granted, Fibonacci
at his word. My torment is
always drawn to scale. I
mean: I appropriate
Pythagoras out of spite. I plant
gardens on my windowsill
and don't ask for more than
they are willing to sprout. I
mean: I tell my friends *I fell
out of love* and that is reason
enough.

## We Moved out of the Projects and into a Home

We painted the walls. Caught mice. Stained the burners with fire. Flushed roaches down the toilets. Left dents on the steps from our falls. Turned solemn grass into a garden and planted a Christmas tree in between concrete. Hung our faces on the walls. Bought a baby chick and gave it a room. Put a bed in the back room and called it Felix's room. Set up playpens for strange babies. Stored toys in the closet in case they came back. Carried mint leather couches up the stairs. Baked birthday cakes at midnight. We painted the walls. Scratched the steps with fingernails and rushed shoes. Moved the chicken to the yard. Ate dinner on folding trays. Prepped pasteles on the dining room table. Rollerbladed on tile. Grilled hotdogs on the stove. Put a TV in the back room and called it Eddie's room. Left dollar toothbrushes under the sink. Washed our bodies with Irish Spring. Cut pork and grease into the counter. Moved the chicken back into the house. We painted the walls. Left out keys and broke glass. Scented the halls, the beds with garlic. Sat on the prickly rug until the power came on. Hid cosmic brownies under our tongues. Spilled brown malta on white carpet. Turned a box of grass into a park. A hose into a community pool. We painted the walls. Prepared a room with infinite warmth. Gave the chicken away. We hung our faces on the walls.

## Twisting Demara's Hair

I said, *Demara,*
*I've never twisted*
*anyone's hair before,*
*not even my own.*

And you said, *That's*
*okay. You'll get it.*

So I decided that I would get it.
And I obeyed the science of getting it.

We drew the curtains.
We skipped the pregame for this.

I studied your oiled grid of banded hair,
held your sections like stalks sprouting
toward budtime. I divided one into two.
Mapped one onto two.
*Grip. Turn. Duck. Grip—turn—duck.*
I gripped and turned and ducked.
The bones in my hands grew sore
so I knew I was getting it.

With chipped nails and artless thumbs,
I pulled kanekalon from my lap,
each strand a bold, coarse scarf
of love.

I watched my hands find their way and felt tender as I counted the hairs on your head.

## First Date After the Breakup

Suddenly you don't seem so cheap anymore.

I track the sun's slow, burning fall through the glass ceiling above and try my best to care about his schedule, the last good book he read, the city he was born in. He holds his stomach full, looks down at the plate in disgust after one slice—though his profile names him a *foodie*—and with that: the twenty pounds you put on my body were a plush gesture of care. His eyes flirt with my chest as he offers me a bite of his scraps and with that: I grieve the pulling of lint from your awful belly button. I grieve the tickling of your nose against my armpit, the tang of deodorant clinging to your dumb, toothy face. I can tell he likes my bangs, but I can't tell if he knows that it's a wig and with that: I grieve your ode to every wig I lay, glue on my head—*I love this wig, you should always wear this wig.* And I grieve the jump in your humble voice when my wigs and I entered any room you were in. The awe in your eyes, as if I had grown those pink or blue or orange mock curls overnight, all on my own. Each version of me grieves being seen by you.

He feels my distance enough to suggest it's time to get back to dishes, laundry, but not enough to know there won't be a next time. We hug goodbye and I wonder why I opted for strangeness and beginnings over our sweet, dull love. I walk home, unmoved & hungry.

# Evidentiality

I've heard it said that grief should be worn like a nightgown. I've heard it said that if our brains allowed it, we could chew off a finger as easily as a carrot. Several online gurus claim that men only fall in love once, and it is reasonable to assume that I'm not the only woman this keeps up at night. I read in a blog post that tucked away in a closet, an Indiana library stores a fat ponytail belonging to Sylvia Plath. It's been reported that during the months leading to her death, her hair carried the smell of an animal. It's been written that Hughes' art would never have seen rigorism, fame if he hadn't met Plath. It's been surmised that Plath would have seen her forties if she hadn't met Hughes. I read in a snippet of a book that the life of a poet is not to be wished upon children. I've read that the prose poem ought to be surreal or it ought to not be at all. Studies have shown that the water in my city is ridden with iron and lead. The internet says trauma is stored in the body, but it doesn't always say where. The internet says that OCD attacks what you love the most. I've heard it said that the body always fights back. I heard someone sing the words *remember us back then* though it sounded like *remember us backward*. It's been said that the sky is vaster in the Midwest. I've seen it reasoned that Plath was, like many of us, the victim of a system, and we've all just pinned it on the wrong one. I've heard it said that grief is to be moved through—that it is one thing to be the thing, another to feel it.

## Siqui's Purse

Is full. At its very bottom,
receipts and bulletins have
grown uninked, washed, and
wrinkled by time. Its worn
handle droops over its worn
base, and let me tell you—
imitation leather has never
been so thoroughly tested.
In this holdall of fossilized
caramel drops and miniature
bottles of diluted baby lotion,
the odors of pocket change
and menthol drops rival for
claim. It is in this black sac
that our matriarch lugs
around emergency rosaries,
pill boxes, chavitos, una cortauña.
In this world, she has carried
proof of my existence, proof
of my illness,
proof of my insurance.
And I, a girl, have dug
with hopeful hands and
reckless fingertips in search
of a ballpoint pen and instead
found a canteen of water
blessed holy by a priest.
And instead
found that this is where
ballpoint pens go to self-destruct.
Only in this compact universe
bounded by polyester lining
and a rickety wooden button,
can I, a girl
can I, a woman
reach for a red lipstick,

dull and years expired,
press it firmly against my
pale, cold mouth and feel
my lips grow warm
and yielding to its lumps.
Only Siqui—a woman
who knows
the onus,
the sanctity
that comes with being
of use
—can pull out a worn,
mysterious tissue and with no
questions asked, will I give thanks
and blow my nose into its
delicate miracle.

# Bira

> A 15-year-old Ethiopian girl, known in medical journals as "Bira," gradually consumed a mud wall near her home. She was eventually diagnosed with obsessive compulsive disorder (OCD).

The last bell sings and I cannot stand the clean of my teeth. I had the thought so I go for the thought, and the thought tells me to find what I must eat. I promise: I am so good and I am so smart. My mother tells me so. She tells the doctors that nothing bad has happened to me. She says I greed. She says I do not hunger. The doctors sigh, ask, *Why?* Again distended, my stomach is already the host of too many living things, but I obey the thought because I had the thought and don't tell me that you've never done something simply because you had the thought. I am so good and I am so smart. My mother stands firm as a wall between me and my thought. She says that most thoughts only last her a few minutes. She says when I was smaller, she used to place a pocket mirror beneath my nose. Waited for the fog to confirm I was not dead, just asleep. There are so many ways to die. Not so many ways to kill. I love my mother. I love my mother until I think the thought. When I think the thought I love nothing. It is then I fix my tongue a slide, my gut a potter spinning the stuff of houses. (They say I am full of the stuff of houses.) I am good and I am smart. I'll eat just until I cannot stand the scum of my teeth. Until my mother does not mind it. She paces. She says she's done her best with me. All things considered. The doctors nod, ask, *Why?* The tears in my throat are unpicked: I've spoonfed them small stones and I've kept them clean. I've trained away the muck on my breath—why? Nothing bad has happened to me. I had the thought. And who's to say that something of the earth couldn't nourish me?

## Girl, I—

Want to tell you about Prozac. I want to tell you
that it makes my dresses tighter and my hands
tremble. I want to tell you that I'll buy new dresses
but Prozac hands are no joke. I want to tell you
that the compulsions did stop for a while.
It was after a family friend found me
shutting and opening my eyes to the clacking
of her rosary beads. The next evening, she
walked me to a strange church in a basement
below a bodega,
where a Pentecostal priest stood before a crowd,
laid hands on heads.
And a woman who sat perfectly fine
on the bench in front of us suddenly flopped
against the cold, white floor like an unwieldy
fish. She thrashed about until her body decided
it could no longer be our spectacle. Then she just
laid there. It was the only time living and dying
looked the same to me. Another woman leaned
into my shoulder, said *it's okay, go up to the altar.*
I didn't go. I just swallowed it all. Until every itch
for control swam against my gut like wild bait
pretending it wasn't born to die. I didn't need a
writhing catharsis, just needed the warning.
I now know how to drown each peculiar
version of me until a new one rises to the surface.

# Ode to Plantains

here's the thing / i'll take you / as you are / in any form / boiled / flattening / to sweet mush / on eager tongue / oven baked / and odd / but most of all / fried / smashed or / fried again / :after i've taken the sharp knife / to your back / sliced you / in diagonals / or small round / cakes / placed you down / in a grease bath / i know sugar / is superfluous / but i like to have fun / and i'll only add / never remove / from you / not your charred / perimeter / candied with glaze / and starch / not the black seeds that line / and cluster / your flesh / my friends / send me photos of you / before buying / because who knows / you better / the superior fruit / yes you are / self-contained / self-sustained / as the jíbaro / who chooses you: / you've never known / the hindrance of seasons / the weight of water / how can i call you / cooking banana / when only you know / what it means to rot / in soft glory / barbaric fruit / soothed by a smoking pan / you've fed me / for almost thirty / years / i'll prepare you / for my best guests / my grandmother prepares you / for me / simple fruit / staple food / remind me that / i love / remind me / what is love

## My Friend,

There is a wig you wear and you wear it often. Yet
each time I see it on your head I ask, *Is this a new
one?* Each time, so excited I swear—this is how other
people talk of their friends' new tattoos, new dresses,
new shoes, new children. You tell me time and time
again, *No this is the same wig you always see me in.*
You remind me each time, though I never ask, that
this is not, in fact, a full cap wig but a lace front wig.
You proclaim that you simply have chosen to tuck
the lace in, under itself. You do it because you don't
care for the hassle—the tint, the glue, the heat, all of it.
Each time I say, *Oh, really?* Each time, you're annoyed,
but each time we laugh about it. And the thing is,
my friend, each time it does look different. Each time
you brush it out to eliminate the tangles inherent to
an everyday wig, its waves land somewhere new
on the spectrum between deep and loose. And I'll
admit—it doesn't always look *that* different, but
maybe like a cousin once or twice removed from
the previous simulation of wig. And it's amazing:
how many times we've sat together like this and
divided time, worry, fish, a bill. How many times
I've shown you my teeth and you've softened
your gaze toward the prey in my gaps.
How many times we've agreed to get on the same
train at two different stations and still
haven't managed to land in the same car.
How with each stop, we run out, exit and enter
one car after the next until we converge
somewhere in the middle. And it's incredible.
Really it is. How we morph with intention
and how we morph when we don't intend anything.
How we can fool the world. How you've fooled me.
How we go through so many iterations of life
together and yet there is always grace to be given
and a laugh to be had. How amazing—really.
To be a witness each time to each and every
unchanged version of woman that you are.

# Forgotten Wig Ode

after Beau

spring cleaning
there it is

in the back of my closet
a pile of hair

capsized
its stretched strap

exposed its laced
front cupping the

ground its whole
body a paused mop

in this one spot
God only knows

how long it has
been there someone

said it was a wiggish
wig and that wasn't

a good thing someone
said it was fit for

a diva it was the
stuff of drama

and that wasn't
a good thing one

man said he didn't
care for it although

he didn't know what
grew beneath it another

said he loved
me regardless said

he'll take what he
can get

a white man said
he didn't even notice

i'm not sure
which is

worse you know king
louis XIV shaved his

head his thinning
hair each morning

so his lace front
wig

could have the
perfect fit you know

the people (his people)
styled their hair

to look like the king's
lace front wig

you know in ancient
egypt if you were poor

i mean lower class
you might make your

wig out of palm
leaves wow imagine that

*my wig plantbased*
*my wig vegan*
*my wig so natural*
*my wig so botanical*

imagine *my wig*
*a whole food* or

*my wig earth-*
*brewed* back then

if you were
wealthy you'd have

two wigs well i am not
wealthy and i have twenty-

two wigs and i don't plan
on stopping there i am

not from ancient egypt
but i will pluck leaf

after leaf until i know
nothing of the sun

i am not a king i am
not a people but right

here and right now
i will bet on

something incredible
decide it gets

to be ordinary
wield it over one

head
then another

## Tabitha,

I'm on the floor again, and that isn't a metaphor for rock bottom. My new therapist asked me how I did it. How I managed to keep myself safe all these years. For the first time in over a decade, I was honest: I don't remember. The meds are working, too, I think. Though after they unfurl my wild patterns, my dreams of precision, all the rot turns to tremors in my hands. It feels like the world ended when we were fourteen, and after years of dodging the undead on bare feet, I finally found my way to cold water and clean shoes. So after the session, I went out and bought stamps: I was thinking of the last time you and I shared a meal. How we cried in the rollercoaster line down at Busch Gardens because we were hot and hungry and couldn't fit ourselves to girlhood. How you said that Tampa will never be home because we wear fewer clothes here and our sweat smells different here. That night we tossed curse words across the dinner table and stuffed our mouths sour with lettuce. —By now you must know that I've broken my promise: I'm dealing with men so I don't have to deal with myself. I'm thinking of one who lives on the west end of the city. He makes bizarre music and I pretend that it's subversive and I pretend that it inspires me. He calls me the poet of silence and hair—you'll be proud to know our love never reached flesh. Thank God it stopped at the bones. I hope you've kept your promise. And I hope your thyroid is better. Tabitha, if I could carry it all, I would.

## Lessons from My Grandmother

1. if you're running low on detergent, just add water.
2. it is your father's job to always look for you.
3. it is yours to not wander too far.
4. when the devil whispers in your ear, stomp your feet.
5. there shouldn't be too much space between your toes.
6. your cousins are always lonely. call them.
7. if you are able, walk.
8. wearing bras to sleep can cause breast cancer.
9. rural Iowa is reminiscent of Puerto Rico, but the South Bronx is as close as we'll get.
10. it is essential to tie a plastic bag over your hair when cooking fish.
11. you don't get smart by going to school.
12. if you can't find your keys, think of Saint Anthony, pray like Saint Anthony.
13. Los puertorriqueños no usan calcetines. Usan medias.
14. if a man has dirty ears, he's no good for you.
15. glaucoma can't stop wild women from sliding thread through needles.
16. don't walk around the house with bare feet. arthritis is always watching.
17. it is your father's job to outshine your mother.
18. it is your mother's job to outshine your father.
19. you should be nice to Padre Ramirez, Padre Eladio, Padre Diaz.
20. they shouldn't be too nice to you.
21. beware of stray uncles, broken glass, and bare nalgas at Orchard Beach.
22. *Y que ten cuidado con los perros, guau guau guau.*
23. sundays are for 11 o'clock mass and cold-cut sandwiches.
24. your nativity scene should be more grand than the tree it sits under.
25. the day you get your first period, you deserve a chocolate cake.
26. but only after you've called every woman in the family to tell them that you have come of age.
27. Los puertorriqueños no usan mochilas. Usan bultos.
28. if you're running out of detergent, mix it with dish soap.

29. the women from church who smell of dried roses prayed for you before they knew you.
30. everyone wants balloons on their birthday. the ones that shine, plump with helium.
31. when you're bored, take a trip to *el 99* down on Simpson Street. go wild.
32. make sure you lock the door before leaving the house.
33. now check again.
34. don't buy from the coquito man. where does he wash his hands?
35. when you do buy from the coquito man, because you surely will, only ask for coco.
36. *No tienes que pasar tanto tiempo por la calle.*
37. grandmothers may fill their boredom with worry.
38. grandfathers may fill theirs by being useful.
39. you can't receive the Eucharist if you've eaten within the hour. put down the coffee.
40. *No éramos campesinos. Somos jíbaros.*
41. the only sleepovers safe for girls are at broken homes.
42. there is always time to pray, and there is always time to cook.
43. *it don't matter if your foods touch.* it's all going to the same place anyway.
44. a clean house exists only in the fourth dimension.
45. when your mother forgets to blow on her hot food, yell *abre!*
46. and blow on the pile of mush sitting on her tongue until she can laugh again.
47. you don't need friends. your mother is your friend.
48. if someone compliments your shirt more than once, ask if they want it.
49. a meal without rice is no meal.
50. we mourn the deaths of Double Discount and Conway.
51. we don't buy chips for more than 25 cents.
52. we know when it's time to go home.
53. it is *always* a little cold outside. carry a sweater.
54. when mami works late, we stay up.
55. if you run out of detergent, use hand soap instead.
56. be patient. the bus will come.

## *@PreCiOuSMeG737*: P. Rivera, If You're Reading This: I Don't Love You Anymore

Never did. I only wanted to know what it might feel like to love a boy. To love a Pentecostal boy, because all the other boys were Catholic, like me, and that is just so, so boring. I only wanted to tell you that it was okay if you were bad at school because I was good at school, and that meant we were a perfect match. Your best friend loved my best friend, so why couldn't you love me? No. I didn't love you. Never did. I loved Damian, actually. The boy who sat in front of me in home room. The one you only spoke to when you got that taste for bullying. Well, one day, I added Damian on AIM because I wanted to provoke him, too. I wanted to have an upper hand like you. He and I instant messaged all night, every night. Talked about mothers, homework, even hinted at angst. He'd ask what size bra I wore, and I'd ask him who he loved. We swapped links to tampered Wikipedia articles, enjoyed the ease of creating misinformation. *Damian Wells served as the first president of the United States from 1789 to 2006.* Our edits were gone by the morning. We never spoke at school. That was the only place Damian reminded me that I was weird and unwanted—your rejection was unrelenting and ubiquitous. I watched you play ball at recess, studied your face as you looked down at your graded test paper, hoped you weren't too sad.

—P., I loved you from homeroom to dismissal. But afterwards, I loved Damian. I sped home every afternoon, anxiously waiting for the desktop to power on, for his screen name to go green. *@damiandamian.* One night he sends a long, indecipherable hyperlink. When I click it: a Wikipedia page—my very own. My whole name: *Meghan Malachi*. The page was nearly blank. No personal life, no filmography, no accomplishments. Just a single line under my biography section: *Damian's girlfriend.*

That night, Damian stopped messaging me. The link was broken by the morning. After 8th grade, Damian went to *that* high school. After that, the army. Lives in Hawaii now. I should have loved him instead.

# Getting a Root Canal on Tooth #15

In my mouth
the orthodontist
turns up an earth
of spit and gunk
with miniature metal shovels.
And while she knocks
frailty into unfeeling,
I, for the very first time,
consider the numbering
of my teeth, their lapped,
American ordering. The *two*
or the *seven* my mother
keeps in a small box,
alongside, touching
my baby stud earrings
and maturing
bonds from 2004. Listen—
when my first set began its topple,
I learned to sleep with the evidence
of loss under my pillow and woke
to a dollar bill in its place:
we celebrated death
those days. Today
my second molar is regal,
crowned with indifferent porcelain.
And rather than savor in its promise,
I ponder the insurance, the price
paid for neglected gums, genetics,
lemon drops post brushing,
cuts of beef fat post floss,
tequila blanketing my incisors
the night I left a bad man for
a good one, chili powder marinating
a rough pit that has finally
come of age, my midnight jaw
sharpening tissue, my back gaps

filled hours too long
with memories of a fine meal
after a terrible day. This
was my second and last chance
and I blew it.
I consider the mechanics
of selfcare while disease
is removed piecewise
from my mouth.

## St. John Chrysostom

At St. John Chrysostom School, we throw fortune teller origami at our friends, and teachers throw desks, slam phones so hard the receivers hang off the walls by their wires. At St. John Chrysostom School, everyone knows that two rings of the bell means that recess is almost over. Three rings: recess has ended. A continuous ring: *fight.* At St. John Chrysostom School, students line up, single file, to buy non-brand pretzels from teachers: 25 cents a rod. One dollar for the whole bag. At St. John Chrysostom School everyone fears that one nun. My oldest friend calls her *the ruler with a ruler*—though, to be fair, Sister Blue Eyes hasn't used corporal punishment since 1999. At St. John Chrysostom School, a new history teacher emerges every three months, but Sister Mary will be principal forever. At St. John Chrysostom School, some of us dread damp milk cartons at noon while others are mysteriously pulled from the lunch line, only to reappear at the end of a long table, exiled and milkless. At St. John Chrysostom School, it costs 5 dollars to dress down on Fridays—everyone always remembers the ones who show up in uniform. At St. John Chrysostom School, us girls get our first gig cleaning chalkboard erasers. We extend our arms over the fire escape and *clap clap clap* as white dust explodes and settles onto our clothes, into our lungs. We never got paid. Got fired after a week for having too much fun. At St. John Chrysostom School we rewatch *Romero* (1989) every year, in every grade. We mourn the archbishop. Shrink at his execution. Perform our annual rage. The following year, the same nun will roll in the same television. Pop in the same cassette tape. And we will ask our memories to spare us ruth. We already know how this story goes.

## The first time I drank too much,

A friend carried me home
laid me down on another
friend's bed stuck her pointer
and middle finger down
my throat
& told me this was the only way I'd be okay in the morning
& fed me a flat ham sandwich
& smelled the bag of vomit just because
& assured me that my vomit didn't have a smell
& then said it happened to everyone
& then ate a palmful of oreos
& didn't even wash her hands first.

## Interview

after José Olivarez and Safia Elhillo

*where are you from?*

As a kid, I never knew how
to properly talk about race. I was a Black girl
and I was a Puerto Rican
girl and we all seemed to think
there was only
one way you could be those
two things at once.

*where are you from?*

Malachi. *Ma-luh-kai.* Biblical.
"my messenger." The last of
the twelve Hebrew prophets
who foretold the coming
of Christ.
In the year 1880,
49 Malachi families were
living in the state of South Carolina. A long
American history
of mispronunciations—*Mala-key,*
*Mal-a-chee.* The stage host calling out for
*Ms. Meghan Mariachi* at the podium
has long left me incapable
of hearing the soft in its volta,
its easy plunge off the tongue. *Malachi.*

*where are you from?*

*Morena*. Black girl.
But my high school Spanish
teacher, a young Polish woman,
says this means *brunette.*

She uses it to describe herself,
so it no longer describes
me.

*where are you from?*

Brigantty. Briganti. Variation of
*Brigante.* Blue-eyed jíbaros
and brown women populate the
family tree. A man named *Hipolito*
becomes *Tony* & if I look close
enough, focus on the smallest
of branches, I find my face. *There!*
There
I go again.

*where are you from?*

I don't believe in nation
states but I believe
in The Bronx. I believe in the line
between Hunts Point and the South
Bronx and I believe that line is firm
and I believe that line is
the Bruckner. My city owes
you nothing. It never
owed me either.

*where are you from?*

- Nuyorican
- girl,
- descendant of Louisiana
- Creole
- descendants of
- slaves.

Someone asks
*where is your accent?*
I lost it
somewhere between 65th and Lex
and Providence, Rhode Island
between Providence and Coralville, Iowa
between Coralville and the very north side
of Chicago
I lost it.

*where are you from?*

I occur among poultry
and blood at the vivero
on Jerome Avenue
the incline up Freeman Street
the right turn onto Hoe Avenue,
the creased leather on Mad Mark's
shoulders, the chain
around Big Pun's neck,
the squeak
of the wheel of the cart
I push around what feels like the last K-Mart standing.

## The Iowa State Fair

Every year at the Iowa State Fair,
held in the city of Des Moines, Iowa,
twelve or so women enter the
husband-calling competition.
Far more charming than
their nearby counterparts—
men, mostly, chanting snorts,
squealing a *pig pig pig-pig piggy,*
their noses digging, dug, deep
into an old microphone
luring dreams of swine to their death—
suburban wives shriek,
yodel, whistle, slander, stomp off
instead.
The summoning of their
*Bobs, Darryls, Johns*
drives the room silent.
Watchers obey and marvel
in their new collective name.

This year, one woman, a fortieth-time
contestant, is dressed in all
white sans a purple bouquet
pinned tightly to her church hat.
She releases a splitting roar
for the late *Roy,* then plummets
into a low, vicious plea:
*You know I love to dance.*
Watchers grieve and accept
their unnaming.

The woman wins it all: the ribbon,
the applause, the five-dollar
cash prize. All the years I lived
in Iowa, I never once made it
to the state fair, never once swiped

or gripped the flesh of its butter
cow. Never burned in exhilaration
for its Iowa twinkie or dove in head
first like an oreo
toward batter and grease.
All I know of this state
is that you either hold onto it firm,
barehanded, upright as a pitchfork,
steady as catfish on a stick—
Or you leave it behind,
let it murmur, blare
like a heart
or a wife.

# Girl, I—

*Can't marry him*, I say.
*That's okay*, you say.
It's decided: there will be no union
of families at a backyard wedding on the
western side of Safety Harbor, Florida.
*I could tell you were unhappy*, you say.
So you scrap plans for your famous pork
shoulder and yellow rice to feed twenty-
five guests. *How could you tell?* You
harden your tone—as if I'd asked how you
knew that the sun would rise or the
night would fall. You tell me who I am. You
tell me when the acuteness of loss has met
its bounds. When I was young, you ushered
me out of the spirals with bowls of cut fruit
and a new baby chicken. Now I am a woman
and we are on the phone and you ask,
*Why are you crying if you don't love him?*
You repeat yourself, and with each echo you
unbuild a heavy load, begin to restore
what I've lost. *Why are you crying*
*if you don't love him?* We hang up the phone.
The next time you call, you make sure I eat
something good for dinner, even if it is only
your voice that pushes the knife, the meat
into my hands, your instructions that move
me through the dark, cold kitchen. We hang
up the phone and don't talk for weeks.
You ask about him once at Thanksgiving.
Once more at Easter.
And then never again.

## WIG

why do you wear wigs
why are you wearing a wig
is that a wig
is it real
why do you have so many
where is your hair
why is it so big
does it smell
what does it smell like
how many wigs do you have
what happens if you brush it
what happens if you don't
where did it come from
who did it come from
are you losing your hair
do you wear that wig every day
why does it look real
why doesn't it look real
do you have good hair
how much did it cost
does it fall off
if i touch it will it fall off
why would you cut it
does he like that wig
what does he say about your wig
do you think it looks good
does it talk to you at night
how do you put it on
how do you take it off
do you wish it were yours
do you know it's not yours
do you sleep in it
do you wake in it
where do you keep it
where do you hide it
do you wash it

do you need it
do you love it
do you love you

## How It Works

Everyone in Iowa City wants to be a poet.
Yes, everyone. Yes, even you, even me,
even the stray dogs and the fallen ginkgo berries.
Yes, even the pigs that outnumber the people
and the corn stalks that outnumber the pigs.
Even the locals who say *what's the big deal?*
and the transplants who answer *nothing, nothing at all.*
Even the sidewalks which erupt into words,
and even the poets themselves.
Even the mathematicians who rip poems
out of anthologies so they can hang them
on bathroom walls.
Even the taco pizza, a symbol for whatever
you'd like it to be, and the cornhole boards,
stray and frequent, begging to be fed.
And even the plain and timeworn bars,
the spontaneous coup by trombones and
drums on game day: footsongs pummeling
through tables—delightful and off-the-cuff.
And even the hipster shops which once
were hipster shops, which once were hipster shops.
And even my perpetual uber driver, who smiles
at the country in my eyes, so sure that I,
like him, *must be Egyptian.*
And even the murals we hide like affairs in dark alleys
and the parking meters that turn dim on the Sabbath.
And even my students, who know that poems
ought to mean different things to different people
but quarrel over metaphor anyway.
Even the comics, who say that Chicago
is just like this but bigger.
And even the vending machines that spit out infinite
poems instead of candy bars and refuse to take
your money no matter how many times you return.
And the dream van, plump with books and films
so old you can't remember what they taught you,

only how they made you see yourself.
And even the storms we watch from open windows
And even the lawn chairs rooted
by the absence of our fear.
And even our love for something interesting, bold enough
to ground itself in a flyover state.
And even the protests that turned into parades
and the parades that turned into vigils
and the vigils that turned into stillness
and even the river
and even the river

# Ophelia

I've optioned to die toward the sky.
    What I leave: a building, hot mouth brimmed with bees and air.

See it: a rose at the hem of agency.
    Tell it: We lived to bedeck the days of a hundred humdrum men.

I'm the heroine. I'm the heroine.
    I won't be left to hold love's screeching child.

They'll position me somewhere between holy and profane.
    All I wanted: to flirt with mud and beauty.

Unhitch my lace from the offshoot.
    You've learned to break language because of me—
    you owe me this much.

## Ode or Anti-Ode to OCD

I want to say you arrived in slow chromosomes that finally got it right. I want to say you arrived fully fleshed—and you did: surprise fish in the sink, sap in the mattress. I want to say that for years we've twitched my body to sleep. That we exhausted ourselves, chose the dark in avoidance of the mantras, the sticky. I want to say you're my gut's biggest pretender, puppeteer in the shadows. You breathe in me and I let out only for you. My hollow mouth is latched to your brimming tit. I'll say it: you've fashioned me a burning stove fanatic, a collector of trash, a tapping woman and colossus of regret. You've retaught me every lesson, yardstick to spine, palm to ass. I've flicked a light switch to its limit for you. I've turned prayer into purity, numbers into idol for you. So when you drifted into a mysterious lull, I held you up, slapped your cruel, dying face. I didn't run into the arms of uncertainty. I brought you back, questioned you back—kept you to myself. Decided you were my nook, my primitive. The sudden joint in the fist of my life. You static, pithy bitch—we came up together. I'm sorry I didn't know how to kill you. The body has no owner. It never could tell what was natural and what was learned. So it made too much room for you. Here—*here*. There is a room for you.

# The Dance

Everyone will let you know that you could dance better.
    No one will tell you that the dance wasn't made for you.
Sixty percent of the choreography is *hair.*
    The soft slouch forward is meant to look *sexy*—
The twirls, not girlish, but carnal.
    And your long, black horse hair is the star.
Its tresses lift: flirtatious and sleek as a skirt.
    Where they land is nothing to you.
A head of locks thrown: over scalp, gripped against cheek and jaw
    to prove: you're fierce, you're in control.
You're feminine and you know it.

Except your hair has never met your shoulders.
    Your hair has never known length, only width.
Never stature, only girth. It doesn't rise thin as smoke.
    It doesn't cave to hands: only water.
It spans.
    It spans!
Your hair will never flip on its backside.
    It is alive.
It holds against weight, carries its own.
    It doesn't shield your mistakes, your faulty rhythms.
That is no job for your body's most tender part.
    It does not part. It does not dance.

## Queen of the World-Wide Web

Behind the screen I was girl I was monster. After school I ran home I logged onto the desktop computer and called my best friend a whore. My mother scolded me, not yet knowing I'd said much worse things before and after that. I rolled my eyes, not yet knowing that years later, someone would tell me, half-joking, *Meg, your digital footprint is insane.* I right-clicked, hit save on photos of boys in my class, uploaded them to strange websites, watched the progress bar crown toward the birth of our cyber child. I typed my teachers' names into Google, printed out their headshots and passed them around recess like war-time propaganda. I watched my ranking fall on Katharine's MySpace page, watched it oscillate between seventh and eighth on Christopher's. I watched P. Rivera's profile picture change from outside the gates, too afraid to extend my virtual hand. I learned HTML, manipulated any code if it meant securing the soundtrack of my life's woes. Behind the dull light of the Dell, I fine-tuned my motor skills, dodging bio warfare with the help of menacing koalas and his human friends. Took my favorite teenage crime fighter on mission after mission only to fail her each time. Paid up to $1.99 for singles on iTunes, told my mother *I love you* when the transaction was approved. Perused chat sites to laugh with European men, who smiled in place of English, whose eyes followed my sequined bosom. Learned that the twitches and spasmic shoulder shrugs were symptoms of disorder, vowed to keep it a secret. Searched my name on urban dictionary. Scrolled pages until I found a definition that suited me. Watched low-budget movies on YouTube—the image of slit wrists, a dying girl never leaves me, though the name of the film is forever lost. Discovered forums, inhaled chilling stories of anal waxing and surprise aneurysms—I then promised to confess my sins as they came and I promised repetition until I felt clean. Learned that this was another symptom of disorder, vowed to keep it a secret. Emailed Edith to say I was sorry. Direct messaged Katharine to say I was sorry. I learned that Ugg boot production was inhumane, did a class presentation on it, vowed to never wear them again, and I never did.

## To the Scar Below My Breast

after Sylvia Plath

The pointed underwire of a four-dollar bra taps then slices through my skin. That's how you came to be. Going through the motions, stuffing my parts into their bowls, I didn't even know the threat until it curved out from under the left cup, chugged up the road it dug in belief of bone.

Then you were born: arc of blood restrained. What followed was a squeamish cloud fogging my head. I shivered to the bath. I shivered as I stood under warm water, watched it flood the sick glow of red. I watched the red slip off my skin. I watched my skin reject the red. I shivered to the cabinet. Pressed gauze against your living mouth. Silenced you, patched you up. Lay down. Grieved your body. Held my own. Counted on the night to smother you quietly.

Long, gawdy comma. Crimson pause between my two fraternal organs. Lone parenthesis beginning a dubious story with no end.

Fishhook reminder of flesh,
you follow my form,
you've bolded
my
breast!

## Latisha the Wig,

you're a lot
of hair.

that's what they
say under and over breath
about you.

vicious in volume
gnarled tacky at the nape
unplucked and wide as central plains

and since i care too much
what others think, i thinned
you down
in the middle of the night,
first with kitchen scissors

and then with a comb
that hides a blade
behind its teeth.

i watched your tresses fall
to the ground in a quiet nest.
and still, large you stayed!

no longer a cape of stiffness
across my broad back,
but a hood, a big blowout,
bigger curls:

pretty brown thing
with a pretty blonde
streak—i've worn you
out. i've towed the line

between endlessness
and trickery. between a touch
up and a lie. i've soiled you
with first and last dates,
burnt your shine dull

to gather vanity
to gather men who
claim virtue
claim love
skip town. i've skipped worlds because i had you.

no bond no adhesive is
strong enough to blur
your knots to my epidermis,
to dub
you fully onto my head
like language pure on tongue,

but I let your clips chew their way
through root to clamp onto tangles

and I choose my own adventure
with the tip of the rattail,
and the hunch of a blackening hot comb

sets the border between the countries
of you.

and hints of kinks peak out
to cover the truth about you.

we live the day
we live the night
i scratch, pluck
a strand from the base
of your cap &

swear
my
own
scalp

tickles, recoils.

## Girl, I—

Will never forget the night
you and Mami tag-teamed
my longest panic attack.

When you talked me down
through the small screen
of our smartphones,
watched my eyes swell
in a hilled exhaustion
as Mami rushed to board
the next plane headed
to Chicago.

When you propped me up on the table
so I could watch you finish a puzzle
of a Sicilian landscape and so that you
could watch me, across state lines,
fall in and out of a fickle sleep
and whisper:

*Duermate, I'm here. Duermate.*

When I said I would finally
go shower because
it was the only thing I could do,
and you pleaded for me
to keep the call going. You said
that you would wait for me.
So I did and
you stayed and
you watched
my bed
unmold itself of me.

## St. Vincent Ferrer

They say the city's best secret lives on the Upper East Side: 500 girls in pleated blue skirts and black Mary Janes. At St. Vincent Ferrer High School, upperclassmen arrive at 7:30AM with wet hair, hot breath, white polos, yellowed underarms, and graying collars. At St. Vincent Ferrer High School, the hierarchy goes as follows: the girls who take Latin and trip acid during first period, the girls who take French and talk conjugations over lunch, and the girls who take Spanish and teach it to their friends on the train ride home. At St. Vincent Ferrer, girls from Riverdale don't say they're from the Bronx and girls from Park Slope don't say they're from Brooklyn. At St. Vincent Ferrer, the mathematics teachers play fair and the religion teachers play favorites. At St. Vincent Ferrer, atheist schoolgirls opt for confession to get out of sixth period. At St. Vincent Ferrer, all grades laugh in unison at the myth of *no distractions*—we look everywhere for love: in our lab partners, voiceless men on the internet, our best friend's backlog of crushes. At St. Vincent Ferrer, the gym teacher's teenage son is a celebrity, a light over our ordinary lunch: *may the best girl win*. At St. Vincent Ferrer, Marcy Kennedy pronounces *union* as *onion* and her cheeks glow with a red that lasts till eighth period. At St. Vincent Ferrer, Alissa DiAmato is allowed to skip Religion on the day we learn what *in vitro fertilization* is. At St. Vincent Ferrer, we don't yet see that depression has a stench and its loud funk is what emanates from our lab mates' lockers. At St. Vincent Ferrer, girls are not allowed to wear tuxedos to prom, so we line dance in silk gowns to "New York, New York," pretending that the absence of our peers, our friends isn't heavy and buzzing between our swaying bodies.

## Ode to Melatonin

Gelatin / lullaby / you lull / my circadian rhythm every / night / tuck
me in / warm my back / handfeed me / the night / O, depressed
millennial / supplement of / choice / staunch the flutter in my chest /
the bark in my throat / croon the crook / in my jaw / unclench / the
violence / from my mouth / slow the peeling of gums / and calm the
memories / of blood / on my lips / until I am limp / and dizzy / with
ease / O, contemporary tracker of sheep / remind me / what *falling*
feels like / what it means / to lie between / two seasons / of myself
/ be my cool milk / and blot / the acid / boiling / under my tongue
/ be the fingers / that circle my scalp / and let me rock from there /
promise me / romance and hues of pink / but if need be / give me /
the nightmares / long as you cradle me there / deliver me the dark /
while I pretend / that the aubade behind my eyes is sound / that the
bellyache of your love / is a slow hug / and / that you're just doing
your job / that this is honest / and natural

## Disease

after Gabrel Cortez

Papa Rey's kidneys are at thirty
percent—a sickly countdown
that began before he was born.
He walks with his back pouring
toward the floor, splays grins of
gratitude between bites of
unsalted chicken. He tells his
son and his son's son it's best to
watch their sodium, their blood
pressure, too. After dinner, when
we decide we only have enough
social battery for each other,
Papa tells me about his first date
at McDonalds, he talks of fields
and factories. He kisses the
photograph of his mother, smiles
at me. *It's good you*
*didn't have to work hard like*
*me.* I'm an ancestral prayer
finally answered.

Mama Judy's legs swell with
liquid and we pray dialysis
will stop the heat. She says
the runtime of clean blood is
about two movies long. She laughs
on the phone with family over
shared diagnoses, and I'm
remembering car rides from my
father's house, when she'd pull
over for milkshakes and diet sodas.
We savored dairy and sugar to the
backdrop of gospel and Luther
Vandross. These days she counts
the ounces of water her body
permits. She promises to give me
the full, scientific name of what
eats through her kidneys, what
could be simmering in mine. The
stuff of blood is thick. I can't get
away from it.

# Rosalind

I think I ought to accept myself. The cause, the emptiness, too. Wear it like a stint or a broach. Feed it sweet like a bird or with haste like a roach. The thick of it. The thin of it. I exchanged an idea of a man for another. Made me truer. Made him falser. I traversed courts, woods, worlds for one only to mother another. Where boys will be boys, women never could thrive. I'll ruin every pairing if it means I survive. I'd throw every fickle bride under the bus if it meant love's clock would match my gait. That its savor could chase my tongue. That my verse might choose its fate. I've tried to be a god and I've tried to be the machine. I've reworked one man to forget the one who left me—I'll ruin every poem if I have to: *Orlando, be anew. Orlando, be the man*
*for me.*

# Papa

doesn't say much. we're alike in that way. he sits in the back seat. lets me sit in the front. flags down the ice cream truck. runs back with a vanilla cone. rainbow sprinkles. hands it to me. drives my friends home. drives anyone home. walks the dog. walks any dog that needs walking. collects baseball cards in danish cookie tins. eats one large serving. makes sure the girls stay fed. makes sure the boys stay kind. smacks roaches with bare hands. carries the tray of mice corpses to the trash bin with bare hands. promises to fix the world if it means i won't cry anymore. answered, *A very beautiful woman*, when i first asked, *Who is janet jackson?* carries money so we don't have to. always cashes a check. can't stand a shirt pocket without a clip pen in it. throws nothing away. says the blessing at every family party. sits with me in the silence. looks to me in the chaos. presses soil into the ground so we can have fresh herbs. sends a *Goodnight and God Bless* text every night. always knows when something isn't right. apologizes first. then asks what he did wrong.

## Mathematics Helps Me Accept My Shrinkage

I never thought I'd write
another math poem
after dropping out
of graduate school.
But here I am, asking you
why it might be that the kernel
of a map, a homomorphism,
to be exact, reminds me
of failure. As a first-year PhD,
I thought of the kernel
as an empty box—that wasn't quite right.
A friend taught me to look at it
this way: you hold a knife to that box,
and actually, that box is full.
and that knife can obliterate everything
in that box, no matter how convincing
or strong or unique its contents may be.
That knife is the *kernel* of that box.

These days, when I think about kernels,
if I ever think about kernels,
I like to think of them
more like this: the countless ways
I attempt to braid kanekalon hair
into my own, each try ending with bright
fibers unraveling wonderfully onto the floor.
Or the ranges of strength with which
I wrap crochet curls around my split locks,
praying that twists find their way to knots.
Or the bottles and tubs of
gels jellies and snots I trusted
to turn my kinks into waves,
to turn gravity into a knife,
not realizing that my plans
were doomed, oriented to nothing
from the very start.

# No Lace Fronts in Iowa City

in iowa / city / i developed / an allergy / to metals / stainless / steel /
nickel / copper / all and / any / would make / my top / and bottom /
lips / burn / they burned / red / they flaked / they cut / themselves /
wide open / cracked open / each smile / a breaking / of burnt / bread
/ in / iowa / city / i watched / my face / swell / with pigs' / blood /
and / pigs' guts / i ate / meats / i never / thought / i'd / eat / they were
/ big / so big / and flat / like / the highways / i walked / in search / of
a bus / i took / the bus / any bus / they all / converge / to downtown
/ its sweet / bustle / in / iowa / city / i went / natural / i call it / going
/ but some / would say / i returned / i quit / did away / with / the
texturizers / serums / irons / i looked / myself / in the mirror / real
good / i decided / to search / for wigs / when i was / a kid / i was /
rushed / to the / dominican salon / at the first / sight / of coiled /
roots / inflowing / a woman named / candy / redacted my / scalp /
clean / and bright / but / i find no women / named / candy / in iowa
/ city / i find / no lace fronts / in iowa city / i learn / that there are
/ roads / in this city / you only / know if / you've ever / hated this
city / there are / mathematicians / quarrelling / like lawmakers /
over / slow drip / at any / given moment / in this / city / there are /
poems / so many poems / to write / about / this city / do you know
/ how many / times / i bet against / myself / in this city / how many
times / i chose myself / despite myself / in this city / i love / this
city / the truth is / there is / no city / there is no / tornado / there is
/ no accent / there is only / a twang / or there / isn't / there is only
struggle / or there / isn't / in ~~iowa city~~ / i finally / see that / the light
/ of the microwave / which projects / its grid / against / the kitchen
/ wall / isn't beautiful / because of / misery / my misery / this city /
didn't give me misery / i brought that / here / no / it's because / i've
prevailed / yes / north / of / the center / of / the states / i've prevailed
/ despite / delayed / pains of growth / i've splayed myself / flat /
rugged / ridiculous and / wide / as tenderloin / and i / prevailed.

## Drawstring Ponytail Anthem

swallow my
unfortunate hair

take its scarcity
into a void

where i can
pretend all

that is me is
simply in stasis

while you latch
and pull and

scratch
for crown

for brain,
silly cat

you're a toothy
liar, a prime

killer of skin
killed

and yes. we ought
to color you

*floating*

and yes. i'm going
for a look

& there ain't nothing
natural about it

so pin it.

pin the pretty pony

on the showy
girl

fasten
my dashing

with your bow
and arrow,

that cocked
and loaded gun

i've never felt so
far from desire

as i do when
it's brushing

up against
my neck

pouring down my
back like rain

give some
take some

sprout
converge

like a sun falling
sweetly over water

pick up these thin
genes' thick slack

take me in
with your netting

# Shura,

Alexandra Tatiana Elise, nicknamed "Shura," was the daughter of Assia Wevill and Ted Hughes.

Where you rest
is now known
if not by many,
at least to some,
who understand that
in every event,
you should have
survived. And in
none should your
grave be marked
by a kind stranger,
etched
with your mother's
regrets,
your life's range
a footnote, a slump
in a blazing story.
In every event,
you should
know little of ash,
nothing of legacy,
all of childhood—
fully named,
loved,
claimed.

# Ode to Plastic-Covered Couches

thank you
for reminding me
that i have never
been small
and my body
has never been
quiet. why move
in silence
when i can slide
and stop
to the beat of
pulled
polymer?
unopened gift
of sitting—
thank you
for night sweats
against your
cool, honest body.
ziplocked comfort—
thank you
for clinging
only to cheek
and to limb
and releasing
the rest.
thank you:
for lining
my back with
flowers,
even if
they
only
grow
and die
underneath
your
skin.

## Girl, I—

Confess: I pretended to be asleep in the car
so we could just go home. You agree: it was
time for bed. We share a bed because I've
come to visit for a weekend and a day and
only you can stand me talking in my sleep.
I think you enjoy the conversation.

*

You offer to dekink the knots in my back
Only to pop the pimples on its surface instead.
I say *ouch* and I say *can you please stop* and
you say *let me just get this one* but it's never
that simple and it's never just one.

*

The part of your body that you hate the most
looks just like mine. The part of my body I
hate the most looks nothing like yours. *My*
*mouth is so small, so so small.* It's funny how
genes work. What carries and what doesn't.
An aunt says *you two talk so similar.* And I
both get it completely and don't get it at all.

*

Girl, I find you brazen soft pecky blue girl
it's blue to be a girl in the world it's blue to be
a girl in a family too I find you kind strict
sickening you make me sick you make me
laugh until my whole head is sweltering red
you make me angry the whole day but with me
you share your bed and

*

My furrow lives in your brow and that damn
tone of ours jumps straight out your mouth.
Your eyes are so wide they carry brown just like mine.

## Straight Backs

Seeing my grandmother for the first time in two years, I lean down to hug her and say, *I dyed my hair.* Her own is hidden under a brown beanie, but I know it is about half an inch long, picked out into a thin afro. She breaks into a smile heavy with guilt for lost time and says, *I know. I know your hair.* No one knows my hair. One day she took me to the salon—I was young, young enough to believe that my hair wasn't a problem. Young enough to believe that hers wasn't either. Right before we walked in, I pointed to the glossy poster of a white woman with large, shining, blonde curls and said, *I want this style.* I looked her in the eye to make sure she knew I was serious. *Sure*, she said, and four hours later I walked out with four clean cornrows a few inches shy of my shoulders. Sometimes I think about how after leaving the salon, the first gust of humid air would've slapped those grand rod curls into limp waves—how the dense efforts of setting spray, serums, and oils would've proven futile. How a drop of rain would've undone the 390 degrees of pressed heat, the wonder of the wand iron, the promise of beauty. How I would have laid awake in bed all night, every night, adjusting to a stiff neck to protect that beauty. Sometimes I think about how long those cornrows lasted, how they survived weekly trips to Rockland Pool and spontaneous darts through fire hydrant showers. How they withstood repeated tumbles through waterslides and the brusque slap of wind on roller coaster drops, the only casualty being the field of frizz haloing the top of my head. How I forgot about curls all summer. How I forgot about beauty all summer. A summer heavy only with water & ease & being.

## Cutting Mangoes for AJ

I've never felt so sure of a world
better off without me in it
until that accent—
flutter against my austere seasons,
village of sweet vowels
pummeling                drawn long
and long jawed,
a real Southside ditty,
—pours through
the other end of the line.
It loves me.
It reminds me that it is summer in Chicago.
There is fresh fruit somewhere.
The day's mouth has just opened
and its caws are so wide.

## Collage

Free will and the thrill of a glue stick
is all it takes:
a punctured, brown
nose sits on the baby cow's face
and a vintage man in a three-piece
suit is branded with poems across his
chest and in place of blood,
confetti looms over the knife's dull
party and I've grafted fauna
onto flora and a gown of angelfish
onto my youngest cousin
and a necklace of planets onto
my oldest,
not a braid but an exciting
eel sprouting
from her perfect head
and a dog jumps over
the moon and Bronx daughters
are caged in a box of tinsel—I will place
a bow on their heads. I will place
the city of New York
in the fields of Kenosha,
Cedar Rapids' murmur
in the heart of Philadelphia.
In place of steam,
there will be glitter. In place of fire
there will be glitter. In place of rain
there will be bullets. Every cloak
is connected, but please pretend
they aren't. Fix a riot
out of my quiet hands,
a canvas out of a trembling thought.
I've superimposed a camera
onto a wound, an ending onto the
sky, a woman
onto a girl. Anything is a hat.

## Shake & GO

Someone tweeted something about headband wigs being the worst new black woman trend. I want to cackle and say it was a flop. A *tweet's not loading* moment, an unfortunate opinion followed by an unfortunate drag. But the tweet has upward of 20k likes. Plenty of retweets, a choir of concurrence in the comments. Well, I and two other women on this bus would have to disagree. My twenty-dollar quickweave is synthetic, yaki-straight, color #4, length right below my shoulders—and it is *bulky.* A whole bulge of cap protrudes from the back of my head, like my brain is swollen with hopes of extra dimensions and hair. I'm not sure how much I care, how much it matters. I wanted beauty and I wanted easy and I landed somewhere in the middle. So when I get home, I relieve my flat feet from three-year-old shoes. I undo the seventh way to re-wear a corporate blouse. I reach toward the nape of my neck, loosen the drawstring I carefully hid under the headband at 6:30 in the morning—I tug the jagged mini combs out from their posts. I throw my hair onto the dining chair, the back of the futon, the bed. I throw my hair onto the hamper, over the TV, onto the dresser. I hang my hair over the doorknob, over the towel rack in the bathroom. I hurl it atop the microwave, wait for its timid jump at the timer's end. I stuff it under the front door, hope it blocks out the draft. I let it singe a bit on the stovetop, sit in the smoke of its foul incense. I toss it over the lampshade, remove my tights under its intimate, dull light. I don't worry about where it should go or where it might end up. Instead, I anticipate rosewater and bar soap, consider what I might eat for dinner.

## Bad Writing

In Complex Analysis, the tall, Danish professor
scribbles conformal maps in blue and punctured
planes in black. His cursive letters blur together
in a strange, mathematical bruise. He paces
in between jokes about Jacobian derivatives,
reminds us that in this world, the opposite of
constancy is infinity is infinity minus one.
What he leaves on the board is a collage
of the day's lesson, new skin overlaying
dead cells. The next class tries to decipher his
artifacts. When they can't, they marvel
at what must be *genius*.

In Real Analysis, the sly, Romanian professor
starts off strong, labels his graphs,
numbers his steps. He feels shy, foolish, even
when he's become too thorough, too clear.
Soon enough, he's running: refuses to prove
a damn thing, only says, *Who stops me?*
when traveling from conjecture to function.
At once, the simple line is no longer
simple and is no longer a line—but a scaffold
for perfectly suited towers,
and it is our duty to rupture them.
Most days, he arrives to class empty handed,
leaves the board untouched, abandons us
to chase his wisdom with our own pens
and paper. We marvel, think: This is what *genius* must be.

In Abstract Algebra, the steady, taut professor
transcribes notes from paper to board
in careful, block letters, coyly slanted.
She scripts the narrative days prior to class
and never lets us threaten it. Tells us,
*Stop writing—just listen.* She reminds us that
these numbers, these numbers we've grown to

love are only symbols and the symbols are empty,
so the algebraist must assume nothing.
In the hallways, classmates whisper,
*She's always so prepared*
*because she's German.* They make bets
on her recitation skills. I attend her class regularly.
She'd sooner us think she is a bad poet
than let us believe that mathematics
makes for
bad poetry.

## Bratz

what a thrill—
to pop out
my ankles,
detach my limbs
for new footwear,
latch hoop earrings
past flesh,
and rock fur
in every season.

oh how I love
to awake
each morning
as a cowgirl,
become a rock angel
by lunch, a beach
babe by night.

*oh!*—to have a hairline
perfectly punctured
from birth
to disposal
and to live in the branded
suitcase of a child,
side by
side with each
of my designated
playmates.

to have a passion
for pout
and to be unlike
the rest of my kind—
to be removed
from puppetry
by a shining mouth,

adequately puckered
and beautifully shut.
to be the curator.
to be the curated.
to be defended
like a possession
or a friend
when strangers
call me out
of my name,
like I don't
already
have my own

*Her name is Cleo.*
*This has always been Jade.*

# Sour

for Coree

When I was six years old,
I dumped a bowl of cereal over
my cousin's head: whole milk,
a spoon, everything. They were
Cheerios, my most and her least
favorite. Icing on the cake.
We were close in that I envied her
and we spent all of our days together,
but also not close in that she didn't
see it coming.

I can never remember what led to that
moment. Why I did it. But what I do
remember is this: she was sitting at the
dining room table, her thin, crooked back
hunched over her breakfast. And though
I knew my grandmother would yell at me
—for the waste of food and the sticky
floor more than the zeal of my anger—
I picked up my own bowl, walked around
the table, stopped right behind Coree Anne
and upturned my breakfast over her
tremendous, open scalp.

Thirty years old now, she cares for me.
She scrubs off the rhinestones stuck to
my teeth after a night out. She soothes
the shell of hardened glue, assures me
that I won't be stuck like this, engemmed
forever. She cleans my teeth for me.
And we laugh about the cereal. She laughs
because I was brave for the first time in
my life and I laugh because despite
not remembering why I did it,
I know her ass deserved it.

## To My Mother, at the End of Spring Break

When we drive up to St. Augustine
and walk in sneakers on the beach
and climb sand dunes in puffy jackets,
I realize that you were right—our bodies
ache less by the water. Your stiff hip
eases against the tide, and the sea breeze
lulls the knot in my neck.
Do you know how good of a woman
you are to make Florida not seem so bad?
At night, we drive until we find churches
and palm trees and more beach.
You tell me to look
out at the water while you watch
the road. And the warm shatter
of city lights cuts across the bay.
You reach over for my hand
and squeeze me into a firm prayer.
I should tell you that you drive
with such easy hands these days—as if
you've spent your whole life here,
in this coastal silence, unknown to the New York
fuss clotting our bones, and I want to tell you
that you make everything better, even this ocean's
stench of fish and death. Even its waters
that clutch at our feet to take us whole.
When we get to the old city, we walk
on cobblestone roads, sand still trailing
our feet. We walk until everything
hurts again. I link my arm through
yours and you carry me, like you always have,
through this life's splitting, beachless winds.

# Common Language

When I decided that I was going
to become a mathematician,
I set out to learn every
math term in Spanish.
Everyone says math
is special
is meaningful
because it's
universal—it's the same
in every language.
But that all changes
when the answers
to questions become
tiny stories of persuasion:
a beginning, a complicated middle,
a victorious ending all to say
*you were right.*
I learned that
convergence was convergencia
curl(x) was rot(x)
antiderivative was antiderivada.
I never learned any other
words, and I never became
a mathematician,
but I learned a third language
—this one here—from scratch,
and from it I plucked
the universal and cultivated
something bizarre
in its throat.

## *Draft*: Girl, I—

Know you don't know me or at least don't remember me. We met once at a bar. You were loud and kind and even though we didn't really click, you said it was nice to meet me and hugged me goodbye. I'm sorry to be writing from a fake profile. I'm sorry to be writing. I wanted you to know that my friend, who you met that night, hit it off with your fiancée. And your fiancée and my friend have become good friends. And your fiancée and my friend go to bars sometimes. And sometimes your fiancée gets drunk and tells my friend that marriage will be a blessing. And sometimes your fiancée gets drunk and asks my friend, who is no longer my friend, to call over those girls from across the bar. Your fiancée has a penchant for girls from across the bar. And once your fiancée touched the small of another woman's back at a party and invited her to his cabin in another state. Your fiancée often invites women to his cabin in another state. Indiana is the state. I know that marriage is a blessing. I know I have no right. I know that we all have a cross to carry. Girl, I'm sorry to be writing. Girl, I'm sorry.

## The Woman Is Fungal

The esteemed poet says the poem starts off gross. There's a line in it about dandruff under my cornrows. *I shouldn't know this. It's effective though.* How do I tell him that he shouldn't know any of it. That we were never meant to know so much of a person, of ourselves. That I can only hope what's inside of me isn't stale. That I can only hope he just can't stand the sight of blood. That I don't wish to write about the men who turn the dry skin of their backs toward me at night. How with practice I learned the topology of each marking, the depth of scratched flesh—their bodies a wall of sleep and avoidance for my musing. No, no. I wish to write about the litter of pale green roaches I found under the five-day old fish sauce. The way they swarmed against my violent sponge, how the strays landed under my pushful finger. The horror lain stiff in my throat. I upturned bowls and pans and mugs in search for the mother. Found her brown carcass floating in the oil. I wish to write about the itch. The day I learned that stress might breach systems meant to keep you safe and a breached system might let in fungus and fungus might cause an itch. And that itch might start in the armpit, spread to the neck, stretch its reach under your belly's flap. This fungus might spread so far as to reach the brain. Now all your thoughts grow a layer of filth. You see things for what they are: Your body has always been a harborer of dirt. Now all you see is fungus. It's everywhere—on the ceiling trickling into your sleeping mouth agape. Under your bed rolling around with the stray hairs and balls of lint. You accept it: You deserve every bad thing that's ever come your way. You are the wrangler of knuckles split and bled. You are the keeper of skin flaking in the crack of your ass. The burns under your breasts will resist all salves but you'll shine in greased pain. The hyperpigmentation between your legs is here to stay. Since you were a girl, you've been called a mess. A hoarder. You were scolded for not cleaning up after yourself, but your friends say they don't mind. They fix up your closets and drawers for you. Still, you try to hide your beast, your savage—throw bath towels over tiers of unfolded clothes, consolidate crumbed dishes into a vertical pile. Your college roommate also doesn't mind. She says your soul is innocent and your room a sin. She likes it. You dated a dishwasher and thought it was a perfect match. He found you lovely and fixable. Then he drowned in a heap of your waste. Still, your dirty habits trailed you city after city. You were destined for fungus, destined to be fungal. One day you stood at your grandmother's kitchen sink, lathered dish after dish, gleamed out the window. You grew watchful of grime, protective of crannies and steel. You felt harmony in the suds bubbling over your nail beds. Felt free of the matter murmuring under them. She kissed your glistening forehead. That night you stepped into the shower, scrubbed the fungus out red.

## Hypotheticals for Solange

Say there is a cut of bile in my stomach.
Say it is ancestral.
Say I'd choke it up to be conversation with you.
Say there is a hand, its palm an offering.
Say I bit the hand.
Say it had no regard for my throat.
Say I've received love.
Say too much of it needed instruction.
Say I've steamed tears into collars, cuffs, hems.
Say I did it cause your airy groan filled the room.
Say I did it cause whatever I'd felt, you felt it, too.
Say I met a brand new word.
Say I wept at the possibility of it meaning both *bird* and *machine.*
Say I've received love.
Say not enough of it followed instruction.
Say I've abandoned sleep.
Say I've opted for a sad figure eight instead.
Say I ticked my waist til my hips went loose.
Say I dizzied myself til the sun inched through.
Say God speaks this language.
Say He *has* to.
Say I pried myself open.
Say it wasn't blood but a man that poured through.
Say it wasn't a man but his nest that poured through.
Say I tend to it.
Say I tend to it.
Say I get the joy.
Say I get the robbery.
Say I, too, choose one in the aftermath of the other.
Say I've tried it all, too.
*Like I get why that one woman thought you were talking about birds.*
*Like I get why I thought you were talking about love.*

## Upon Realizing the Man I Kissed at the Bar Last Night Is Married

There wasn't a ring, but the signs were there.

When he curled his large, firm hand on the small of
my back and said, *Hey, what's your name*, I didn't feel

provoked or trapped or plucked from a drawing of crowded,
sweating bodies—just soft. Wanted. It must have been

the blue lights, the lonely in my eyes, that set the mood.
He said that my glasses were sexy and my slow wine was

cute. That I must be some sort of writer with an interesting
life. That I must be hard to get to know.

His friend's date sized me up, but I ignored it. A man for whom
money couldn't be a thing was pouring over me,

so I ignored her. He was attentive
in a way that filled the template: asked if I needed liquor, juice,

water. With each *yes* and *okay,* he walked dutifully to the bar.
He was inattentive in a way that filled the template: met my eyes

to ask if he could take me out sometime, shifted them
just past me when I said I'd like that very much. He spoke of two

jobs, one on each continent. No specifics or passion, really. Just
sharp, heavy eyes. He talked of second, third dates, even held my

hand. So I joked about a fourth date. Then he let go, like he
forgot who I was, like he forgot who I wasn't. The blare

in the silence was tugging at my hem—I didn't feel it.
The crook in his confidence was forming in real time—I didn't know it.

I mistook it for dwindling interest in my tight dress, shining chest.
The signs were there. His insistence on taking my number, never offering

his. The dim assurance in his voice as he shrugged his jacket on.
*I'll call you, I'll call you.* The limp in his stride, a walk that could
 only come from

a man trying to be excellent or
a man just trying to get by.

## Second Weave / First Closure

It itched until I scratched. I scratched until
it hurt. It hurt until I relented—scissors to
netting, fingernails to thread, hands to bundles,
bundles to floor, 400 dollars down the drain.
Even then, it itched. It flamed and I scrubbed.
I scrubbed until suds
and suds gave way to clogs and clogs
gave way to tears and scum
and even then, it itched some more. So I picked.
So I picked. Because I deserve warmth, I pressed.
I rubbed. I tapped. Yes, I tapped
the absence of my weave. I tapped my
head's crown like a woman at its door. Like
a belt to the backside. A rope to the ground.
A palm to the field spot of a grocery store melon.
Like a second palm to its antipode for good
measure. I tapped it like a humming fly
cracking the fall before it breeds,
like a golden spoon of reassurance
to the rim of obsession's porcelain cup.
It itched and I cried. I cried until mercy came and
The itching stopped and all I had left was relief
and the memory of 400 dollars and the moment
preceding the first itch: *I was stunning.*
Cloaked and untouchable in 24 inches
of bone straight, Peruvian, obsidian hair. In weave
I was enclosed—like something
special.
I was worth the risk.

## *Safety Harbor, Florida, 2020*

My grandmother grows sweet potatoes in her backyard. Basil, taro, tomatoes, something called *culantro*, too. I ask her what that is. She doesn't answer because she doesn't know how to say it in English. And I can't help her because I've never seen this long, jagged leaf in either language. Its name skids off my tongue over and over again, as if repetition might massage the memory. *Culantro culantro culantro.* She hands me half a cup's worth of ají dulce. The bite-sized green and orange juggle in my palm. Their dense musk must have floated through the kitchens of every woman in my life. It hovered over plates of arroz con pollo sat before me. I was a kid well-fed. I was a kid ungrateful for a pepper that could color a pot of rice with every flavor it needs. Today, my grandmother's basil leaves bloom over a large tree and the tomatoes dwell in old milk jugs sliced in half.

Back in the Bronx, my cousins and I would snatch small, undergrown tomatoes off my grandmother's suffering trees. I'd throw the plump red, sometimes green fruit as high as my arms could reach, and my cousin Marc, standing eagerly, knees bent, on the other side of the yard, would swing a bat—right on time, every time. We jumped and cackled under the sudden explosion of seed and juice.

Today, my grandmother rips off a small green pod, opens it for me to see the glossy gandules maturing inside. She tells me to hold them *up up up* toward the sky so I can see the pigeon peas through their casts, perfect and bold in the sun's light. And there they are: three tiny beans in three tiny cells. Two pinching, clenching their stems. One bubbling firm through the womb. My grandfather joins us outside. I ask if he misses his friends from New York, the ones from church. He says, *All my friends are dead now.* He looks out toward the marina, past my grandmother, past me. The garden's tallest plant cranes its neck over the roof.

## An Untimely Ode to Nelly Furtado

Get this: We were the problem.
We likened your nasal cavity
to a window clean open, a door
thrown wide. Called you mother
of the eccentric, blueprint of the
sellout. Both loved and scoffed at
the wings fluttering in your throat.
Legend has it, we can trace
whole genealogies, a hoarse-mouthed
somethingness in even the sleekest
of today's most popular girls ties back
back to your pitch-hitting cursive.

Still—I don't know another who could
groan herself and myself into a rich,
crazed frolic, who could take a walk
from Crotona Park East to Hunts
Point and wrap it in worlds
of folklore, who might sell me pipe
dreams of my own pretty, pluck
out the poem stuck under my tongue
and braid it into my hair instead.

What choice did I have but selfhood
when you planted a green fledgling
at the bend of my youth? Avian Anthem,
Bird Ballad—it all made me feel
gentle and rural and, yes, free.
And yes, sometimes your pivots
upset me. But get this: it's a new age, Nelly,
and the girls are allowed
to mount that multi-trick pony.
And yes, I'm a fan, I'm a fan, I'm a
*stan*!

I've never liked the outdoors very much,
but all I've ever wanted since the year 2000
(and what is more the year 2000 than
that song?) was to lie on the grass,
on my side, and despite my awful and budding,
busty chest, all I've ever wanted
was to lie on the grass, on my right side,
in a fitted orange tank, stiff as a plank,
and whisper a song, waiting for adolescence
to end. Waiting to grow past terrors of
broken single-file lines, a raised hand one second too late,
a running nose, pockets empty of tissue.
Oh, Nelly, when I sing your song,
I can't help but part my hair down the middle,
let the buzzing pulse of grass follow
my scalp road past green, past girlhood.

When it's time to end things,
when it's time to gather my selves off the tile,
to choose the wrong meter,
to write the bad verse,
I fry my own tune til it meets your rattle.
I keep with it until I soar toward loss
and until I'm faithful to no machine.
I revel in the
promise of *early*
and decide that I, too,
might be birdlike
and strange.

# God Willing.

My grandmother is reliable
though she never makes
promises. She agrees, firmly,
to make my favorite meal,
to take a morning walk with me
along the marina,
to visit me in Iowa City,
with the even firmer disclaimer:
si Dios quiere. While there are
countless things on which we
disagree, we both know that
the will of God surpasses our own.
We both know that God laughed
when she said she'd never
knit a blanket for a dog,
when I said I'd never
learn to cook, wash a dish,
bask in the warmth of cooking
a meal that someone else enjoys,
dwell in the comfort of a shining,
greaseless sink.
When we said we'd never
understand one another.
When I said I'd never rationalize
feelings of worry when my mother
doesn't answer the phone,
and I'd never walk back
down the block to check that
the iron was unplugged,
and I'd never wake up
in the middle of the night
to ask a guest if they were
cold and needed an extra blanket.
When I said I'd never inherit
the worry, the cycle of misery,
emphasize the obvious,
state what is implied:
si Dios quiere.

## Girl, I—

Hope you never get too old
to hold my hand as you do
when we walk, anywhere,
side by side. Let's rejoice
in the sweet gourmand of the
perfume you scavenge my
closet for, in the mint musk
of the tea tree oil I lift from
your bathroom counter.
Let's rejoice in the shared
shame of our late day glow.
Reconvene for gossip after
we've had our showers.
With fast hands you clip my
webbing cuticles, bind my
heavy breast with patches
of tape, crochet
new shapes to life, creep
through the bedroom
door to gift me a light pink
star of yarn after a long day
at work. I will be years
cackling through your insults,
sharp and beautiful as your
candy-red acrylics scratching
at my palm's itch. Girl,
I hope that even in old age,
there will be no cupping of
shoulders or linking of
elbows, but a hand in a
hand, fingers bolted sweatily
to knuckles.

# Juanita

Juanita shouts, *I'm summa time fine!* on the first day of summer, and it never gets old. Juanita's skin is kept smooth and dewy by African black soap and two pumps of baby oil, devoutly. Juanita gets chestnut box braids with a splash of blond because she just got paid. Juanita laughs at her own jokes, and she laughs for too long. Juanita says her life is a vacation cause she's going home to God soon. Soon can mean tomorrow or in ninety years. Juanita is a vegetarian most of the time. Juanita hasn't drunk Coke in over ten years. When a tortilla chip is pushed out of the complimentary basket and lands on the table, Juanita picks it up and eats it. Juanita talks a lot. Juanita knows she talks a lot. Juanita has curved, wide hips that never learned a rhythm or a beat but swing a hula hoop for 5 minutes straight, naturally and unrivaled. Juanita wants to live. Juanita doesn't know how to use *finna* correctly. *I'm gonna finna do that.* When I wear my natural hair, Juanita doesn't tell me I look prettier. She tells me I look the way I'm supposed to. Juanita wonders if Sandra Bland liked to eat cake on the first day of summer. Juanita buys us a tiny cake on the first day of summer. The back of Juanita's neck glistens, damp with sweat. Juanita hushes flirting boys when she has something to say. She tells me the thoughts that unhitch themselves from the backcloth of her mind. The way lightskin boys hold their chins in group photos. The lyrics of that one Three 6 Mafia song she finally remembers. *You don't know how hard the life of a pimp is!* Juanita always asks for relationship advice, though she never takes it. She did hair back in high school, so Juanita holds the hair blower at its tip, immune to scorched air. White people tell Juanita she's not ghetto, just innovative. Juanita wonders why both can't be true. The day after a fight, Juanita greets me with guilty dimples and an upchuck of neglected secrets. Juanita scratches my back to help me fall asleep and lets the fan keep in my direction all night. When I give Juanita a kiss on the forehead, she looks at me like I had birthed her. The dull, clear wall of ordinary friendship collapses between us, and Juanita says we're family. She makes me promise. Juanita lets me know my vomit doesn't smell. Juanita tells me I eat a cookie like it's a freakin' sandwich. *Damn.* Juanita braids my hair. Juanita lays peppermint oil on my throbbing scalp and massages every itch into submission. Juanita makes simple dishes—fried plantains, grilled cheese with swiss—and dresses them in beautiful words like *palette* and *savory.* Juanita comes with me to mass and sings off-beat and loud, insisting on tight hugs while the people around us throw two fingers up at their mothers and children. Juanita says we believe in different versions of the same God. I tell her I am better for it. Juanita leans her ear toward my mouth to hear me sing, like a mother does when her child speaks up for the very first time. Juanita says the real first day of summer is when the multi-legged bugs return to your ceiling, mysteriously and right on time. Juanita braids my hair. She rips out the root and sews the seed at the same damn time.

## *Woman at Her Toilette* (1875/80)

I'm reading prose at the dining table and a man in heartbreak caterwauls through the windows. His song pours in with the draft, its roaring refrain a maw of sorrow. I want to tiptoe around it, but after an unjust winter, this day is full of light. The breeze is so tame and I know exactly which coat is best to wear. I wasn't always this way. But it is Sunday. It is a Sunday that is less aligned with doom and more akin to mercy. I've thrown my keys onto the center of the rug so that I don't forget them when I leave—I'd rather bruise the soles of my feet than count on my own memory. The washing machine is working again. It no longer churns coins to flood water and suds. There are pecans glazed and pressed into a loaf of bread. I bite. Last night, a neighbor placed a box full of clinking perfume bottles in the lobby, and this morning I spray a rose eau de toilette over my head. In the mirror, I gather all this hair, stack it onto my scalp's summit and despite the hope of flowers, yeast, soap: I sing along to the familiar tune. How am I supposed to go on while the dark collar of another's misery is tearing into my neck.

## I’m Cleaning My Apartment

because the filth is starting to carry over onto my body. dandruff packed into cornrows pushes past my wig cap, and the night’s sweat tucks itself into my underarms. because walking from the bed to the oven is a trek—bare feet dodge stained underwear and bags of flour like pressure mines. tea bags sprout new life in strange mugs. toilet paper rolls clutter the tile. sand sprinkles the hardwood. there is writing on the walls. toothpaste in the kitchen sink. fingernails swirling the toilet bowl. electric bills in the hamper. poetry under the pasta. the water in my belly is coated in lead, and from the same bottle we drink: me, the diffuser’s frankincense, the succulent, the bonsai, the mop souring its blue bucket. acrylic paint clots the rug—remnants from the night i blended colors because i was never good with sheep. i put on my best skirt and brush a white canvas with pink tulips that stand firm and monstrous. i begin with the bathroom, scrub my skin from the rim of the drain. i shelve brushes and bottles and blush until the echoes of my song grow louder. i am making space. my inner girl clutches my ankle from the tub to the door like a dying dog. my hands jerk the handles of a trash bag and it blooms. we have to live here.

## Loading

In place of tears, I've opted for a glass of ice-cold water. In place of bleeding into my summer duvet, I've chosen a leather chair that rattles beneath me. I finally see my resemblance to my mother, so at the end of the world, I've chosen to live. In place of learning how to fire a shot, I'll learn when to patch a wound. In place of a car or an army tank, I'll find a horse instead. I will run the poems farther and I will look at the flowers. I will bypass all caution tape and corroded gates. I will touch every vine that takes the shape of a large, vicious hand. Celebrate the ground growing vintage with rot. In place of the sun, emerald leaves will hug red brick without bounds like disease. I will remember only the smell of closed palms, cut grass green on my back, my dead dog's yellowing teeth. And in place of cowardice, I'll tell my mother that so much of her has yet to trickle down to me. Yet I wait for it like a due season. Without touch, I will clutch onto anything that fights to be mine. Without language, I will pray for anything that tries to prevail. In place of grief, grace will outstrip my anatomy. In place of shame, I will tuck this ear-length hair into that fishtail braid

I always wanted.

## Girl, You're Puerto Rican

is a common response I hear
when I admit
that I don't like rice and beans,
or rice and peas,
or rice at all, really.
I'm met with surprise,
surprise that ties back
to me being Puerto Rican,
to me being *Latina.*
As if my stomach, or my tongue,
is predestined toward
pigeon peas & chicken bouillon.
I don't like a lot of foods
that many would consider
*Puerto Rican.* Alcapurrias:
rolls of salty funk. waste of plantain,
in my opinion.
Sancocho: burning
hot broth of bone, floating
puddles of oil unabsorbed.
Flan: jiggly rhombus of
sticky and slime. sitting
duck, basking in itself.
What I prefer is this:
Malanga. shaved of its
skin, boiled to a lush, cutting
perfection. Pasteles.
sans raisins and olives.
thick block: chewy coagulations
of plantain, my dear fruta barbaro.
Sorullos. deep
fried corn fritters, crunchy sweet
or crisp with cheddar filling.
what a corn dog would be
if the world were good.

# Acknowledgments

Thanks be to God for providing me with breath, gifting me with wisdom, and surrounding me with love.

Thank you to my confidante, my ultimate role model, my "Thelma"—my mother, Cristina Brigantty. Every good thing I've ever done is because of you.

Thank you to my grandmothers, Francisca Brigantty and Judith Malachi, and all the women in my family, whose selflessness and antics brought these poems to life.

Thank you to my father, Anthony Malachi, and my papa, Reynaldo Briganti, for your love and support. Thank you to my siblings Geena, Ani, and Mikey for your love and support.

Thank you to my thesis committee at DePaul, Richard Jones and Chris Green, who read these poems, this manuscript before anyone else. Thank you for your feedback, your time, and your support.

Thank you to Coree Anne Brigantty, Alexa Cabán, and Maya Cabán for picking me up when I fall, for making me part of something beautiful.

Thank you to Crystalinda Rapozo for being my best friend, my partner in crime, for having my back all these years.

Thank you to my best friends, Aliyah Jones and Christa Prophete, who inspire me endlessly.

Thank you to Isabeau Belisle Dempsey for your editorial prowess and your ever-inspiring friendship.

Thank you to Grace Tsichlis for your feedback and invaluable friendship throughout the MFA (and beyond).

Thank you to Virginia Bell and Rebecca Johns-Trissler for believing in my work and for your mentorship.

Thank you to the following poets, who in one way or another taught me what I know about poetry—without their poetry or their instruction, many of the poems in this book would not exist: Richard Jones, Chris Green, Mark Turcotte, Tara Betts, Ariana Brown, Stephanie Karp, and Andy King.

Thank you to *RHINO Poetry*, *Indigo Sessions*, and *Writers With Attitude* for providing me with community and opportunities to grow in my craft.

And thank you to the following publications, which published several of the poems (or earlier versions of the poems) that appear in this manuscript:

*Black Horse Review, boats against the current, Ethel Zine & Micro Press, NECTAR Poetry, NewCity, Packingtown Review, Pages Penned in Pandemic, Quarterly West, Rabid Oak, Sledgehammer Lit, South Florida Poetry Journal, Spoon River Poetry Review, The Orange Couch, Voicemail Poems*, and *Writers With Attitude.*

## About the Author

Meghan Malachi is a poet and writer from The Bronx, New York. She is an associate editor at *RHINO*. Her poetry collection, *No Lace Fronts in Iowa City*, was selected by Allison Joseph as runner-up of Madville Publishing's 2024 Arthur Smith Poetry Prize. She is the first-place winner of the *Spoon River Poetry Review*'s 2022 Editor's Prize Contest and runner-up of the 2024 Princemere Poetry Prize. Her chapbook, *The Autodidact*, was published by Ethel Zine & Micro Press. She lives in Chicago, Illinois.

www.ingramcontent.com/pod-product-compliance
Lightning Source LLC
Chambersburg PA
CBHW021336060726
47591CB00006B/2054

* 9 7 8 1 9 6 3 6 9 5 6 9 4 *